HUMPBACK WHALE

CUVIER'S
BEAKED WHALE

BOTTLENOSE DOLPHINS

MINKE WHALE

NARWHAL

PYGMY RIGHT WHALE

SPERM WHALES

The Blue Whale

by Donna K. Grosvenor
Paintings by Larry Foster

BOOKS FOR YOUNG EXPLORERS
NATIONAL GEOGRAPHIC SOCIETY

Try to imagine that you are a blue whale.
You are very, very big.
You are the largest animal that has ever lived.
You are as long as three big school buses end to end,
and you weigh more than 30 elephants.
Your tongue alone weighs as much as a young elephant.

But in the water you do not feel heavy.
The water lifts you and holds you up,
so you feel as light as a feather.
And even though you are very large,
you glide easily and gracefully through the sea.

One day, far out at sea, a baby blue whale is born.
The newborn whale looks small beside his mother,
but he is as long as five bathtubs end to end.
The baby whale is so large we call him Big Blue.

He lives in the ocean, but he is not a fish.
He is a mammal as you are, and he must breathe air.
Instead of a nose like yours,
he has two blowholes on the top of his head.
Big Blue opens his blowholes above the water to get air.
He closes them when he goes underwater.

When a whale breathes out, the air in its lungs
whooshes out of the blowholes.
People can see the spray, or spout, from miles away.

Big Blue is a hungry baby.
He pushes his tongue against his mother's nipple,
and her thick creamy milk squirts into his mouth.
In one day, Big Blue gulps enough milk
to fill many hundreds of glasses.
He grows very, very fast
and gains 200 pounds a day.
This is as much as a large man weighs.
At first, the mother always stays beside her baby.
They touch and pat each other with their flippers.
Whales also use their flippers to steer
and keep their balance in the water.

How easy it is for whales to swim through the water!
The mother and baby speed along
just by swinging their tails up and down.
The two flat parts at the end of the tail are called flukes.
The mother dives down into the sea.
Big Blue dives right beside her.
Whales can even swim upside down.

Soon mother and baby will begin a long, long journey.
They will go to their feeding grounds
in the icy waters of Antarctica.
But the mother and baby will not be cold.
Under their skin, whales have fat,
called blubber.
This blubber is like a thick blanket
and keeps them warm.

On their way to Antarctica, mother and baby see
a squid struggling with a sperm whale.
The sperm whale is another kind of whale,
and squid is its favorite food.
The sperm whale holds the squid in its mouth.
The squid wiggles and fights to escape.
But the whale does not let the squid get away.

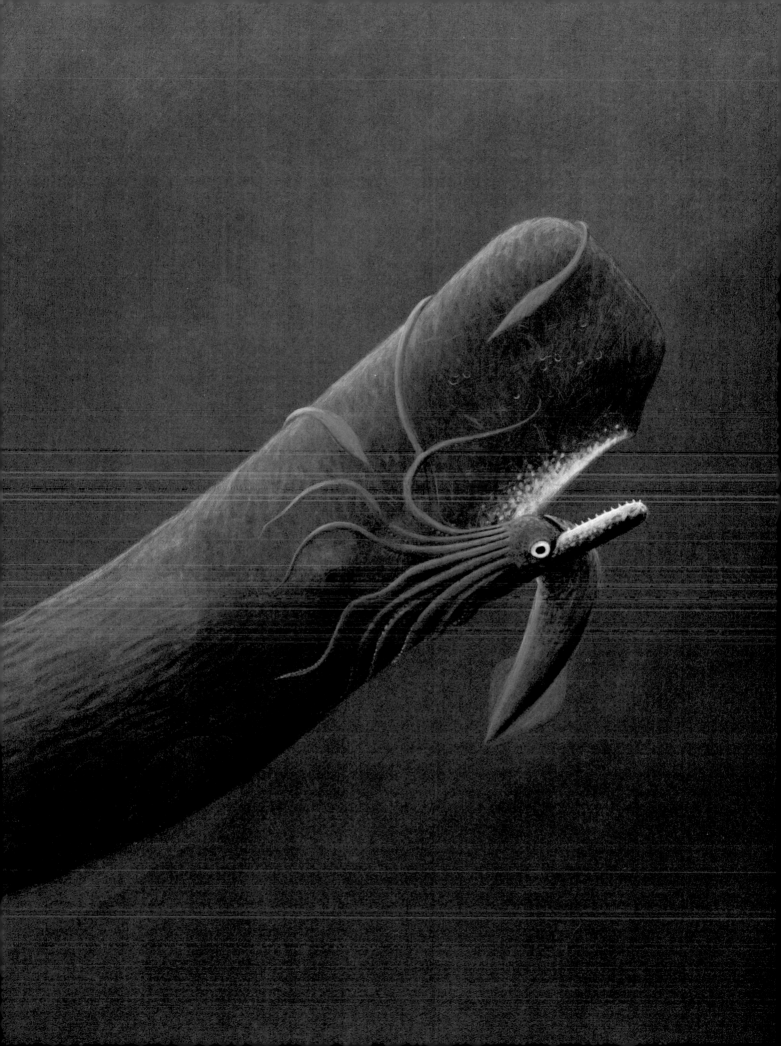

As they swim toward Antarctica,
Big Blue stops to rest and play.
He throws himself onto his mother's back
and makes a loud splash as he flops into the water.
Mother and baby play together for hours.
There are no other baby blue whales to play with.
Blue whales do not travel together in large groups.
Big Blue has only his mother
to keep him company in the huge ocean.

Suddenly, black-and-white killer whales
speed like torpedoes through the water.
Killer whales are also called orcas.
Hungry orcas could mean danger for Big Blue.
These mighty hunters with their big teeth could easily
attack and kill a young blue whale.
But mother hears the orcas,
and she keeps Big Blue safely away.

After many weeks,
Big Blue and his mother
arrive in the cold waters of Antarctica.

Huge chunks of ice, called icebergs,
float in the water.
Penguins waddle on the icebergs like windup toys.
They line up to dive into the ocean for food.

Big Blue will remember his journey.
Year after year, he will swim back to Antarctica
to find the food blue whales like to eat.

Food! At last, mother sees food.
She finds the ocean full of orange krill.
Krill look like shrimp and are about the size of your middle finger.
Mother has had very little to eat for six long months.
Big Blue has lived on mother's milk.
But mother did not find enough food until she arrived in Antarctica.
Now mother will feed on thousands of pounds of krill a day.

There are so many krill in the water
that the ocean looks like thick orange soup.
As mother swims through the krill, she opens her huge mouth.
Her mouth fills with water and hundreds of pounds of krill.
The krill and water stretch her throat until it looks like a big bag.
Instead of teeth, a blue whale has baleen.
The baleen grows down from the upper jaw and looks like a comb.
Blue whales strain their food through the baleen.
When the mother closes her mouth, the water squirts out,
and the baleen keeps the krill inside.
Big Blue takes his first mouthful of tasty krill.
He is now old enough to find his own food.

Swack! Big Blue hears a sound like thunder. It is
the great splash of another kind of whale, called a right whale.
It leaps into the air upside down
and crashes into the water on its back.
The sound is so loud it can be heard for many miles.
The right whale got its name from men who hunt whales.
These whales were easy to catch,
so the men who hunted them called them right whales.
White lumps of thick skin grow on the head
of each right whale. No one knows what they are for.

Even the largest creatures on earth are not safe from danger.
The worst enemies of whales are whalers, the men who hunt whales.
Whalers in boats are chasing these three whales.
When a boat gets close enough, a whaler shoots a harpoon from a gun.
If the whale is hit, the harpoon explodes and kills it.
In the distance, a big factory ship waits to cut up the dead whales.
Men kill whales for their blubber and meat.
They melt the blubber to make oil for soap and machinery.

Some people eat whale meat.
Others use it for pet food.
Today, blue whales are not killed by whalers.
But so many have been killed
that only a few blue whales
are left in the world.
Now people have decided
not to hunt them any more.

A fierce storm sweeps over the ocean.
Lightning flashes across the sky.
Big Blue rides the giant waves
as if he were on a roller coaster.

Big Blue is now nearly a year old,
and he no longer needs his mother to protect him.
He can swim back to warmer waters all by himself.
The time has come
when all the blue whales leave Antarctica.

Mother has made the long swim
to warmer waters.
There she meets another blue whale.
They swirl and weave
around each other.
They are as graceful as dancers.
The new whale will become her mate.

Big Blue is alone—all alone in the great ocean.
In a few years he will look for a mate.
But the oceans are very large,
and there aren't many blue whales left.
Big Blue might not find a mate.
If Big Blue and other blue whales do not find mates,
a time may come when no blue whales are born.

Only people can keep blue whales from becoming extinct.
Extinct means gone forever, and there will never be any more.
People must keep on protecting the blue whales,
so there may always be animals like Big Blue in the ocean.

Published by The National Geographic Society
Robert E. Doyle, *President;* Melvin M. Payne, *Chairman of the Board;*
Gilbert M. Grosvenor, *Editor;* Melville Bell Grosvenor, *Editor Emeritus*

Prepared by
The Special Publications Division
Robert L. Breeden, *Editor*
Donald J. Crump, *Associate Editor*
Philip B. Silcott, *Senior Editor*
Cynthia Russ Ramsay, *Managing Editor*
Elizabeth W. Fisher, Carolyn Leopold Michaels, *Researchers*
Wendy G. Rogers, *Communications Research Assistant*

Illustrations
Jody Bolt, *Art Director*
Suez B. Kehl, *Assistant Art Director*
Cynthia E. Breeden, Lynda S. Petrini, *Design Assistants*

Production and Printing
Robert W. Messer, *Production Manager*
George V. White, *Assistant Production Manager*
Raja D. Murshed, June L. Graham, Christine A. Roberts, *Production Assistants*
Debra A. Antonini, Jane H. Buxton, Suzanne J. Jacobson, Amy E. Metcalfe, Katheryn M. Slocum,
  Suzanne Venino, *Staff Assistants*

Consultants
Dr. Glenn O. Blough, Peter L. Munroe, *Educational Consultants*
Edith K. Chasnov, *Reading Consultant*
Dr. James G. Mead, Smithsonian Institution, *Scientific Consultant*
General Whale, Consultants and Research Assistants to painter Larry Foster.

Library of Congress CIP Data
Grosvenor, Donna K   The blue whale.   (Books for young explorers)
SUMMARY: Presents a year in the life of a blue whale and her offspring.
1. Blue whale—Juvenile literature.   [1. Blue whale. 2. Whales]   I. Foster, Larry, 1934-
II. Title.   III. Series.
QL737.C424G76   599'51   77-76971   ISBN 0-87044-243-0

Whales of the World

PILOT WHALES

GRAY WHALE

RIGHT WHALE

BLUE WHALE

FIN WHALE

SEI WHALE

BOWHEAD WHALE

BRYDE'S WHALE

BAIRD'S BEAKED WHALE